Becoming Her 101:

-Little Life Lessons to Live By-

Tiffany Lewis

www.BecomingHerNow.com

Layout and Design Editor: Meika Louis-Pierre
www.MeikaLouisPierre.com

ISBN-13 978-0692805442
ISBN-10 0692805443

Dedication

This book is dedicated to my past.

While running from you,

I ran straight into my destiny.

Acknowledgements

First I would like to thank God for preparing my gift my entire life. The wait has been so worth it.

To my husband Dean, I told you my dreams and you took out your paint brush to help me paint this beautiful life. Your love is unreal.

To my three sons Justin, Aaron, and Jayden, there are no words I could write to express my love for you.
If doors appear not to be opening for you. Build one!

To my Mom, let's drop the top and ride out into the sunset baby! "Though it may tarry, wait for it."

To Chels my only sister, aka "my girl", thank you for being my "everything" before it was anything. Love you.

Pop, thank you for all your support since the day you entered my life.

Matt, I'm holding the door open for you my little visionary!

To my grandmas Eleanor & Lolita, your first grandchild loves you.

To all my relatives that I cannot list please know that I love and appreciate you.

To Tamiko Lowry-Pugh and Liza Davis, I finished a book from your inspiration. Thank you.

To Jenai Gatlin, thank you for waking up a sleeping giant.

To all my friends, you guys sure know how to love me. I love you all.

2016 was so lit! We're just getting started.

Contents

Introduction

Sitting in front of the mirror, I checked out all my physical features.

My fat cheeks, my slanted eyes, the way my bottom lip hangs down a bit, and that itty-bitty nose I have. A smile graced my face as I began to clean off my makeup. I started with my red lipstick – something I wasn't always confident enough to wear.

Who I was and how I looked didn't always make me smile. Behind all those physical features were pain from my past, mistakes, and failures. There were the whispers of those who'd once told me I wasn't good enough. So when I looked into the mirror, it wasn't with a true view, but through the lens of others.

Makeup is good to cover blemishes of the skin, but it can't cover any parts of a blemished soul. The lies that people place upon you will become your truth if you don't learn the ever-evolving lessons that I have. You must learn to find that special someone to remind you of how great you are. That someone that will whisper sweet nothings to you and tell you how adorable you look. Someone who will look at you and smile simply because of who you are and not because of what you do.

I mean the person you can call on when people have talked about you when you've messed up like they've never made a mistake.

Who is that someone you don't mind being alone with? Someone that you love because they've accepted you with every imperfection that you own. When they speak to you, do they help you feel inspired like you can take on the world just one more time?

I want you to find them and hug them. I want you to squeeze them tight and say thank you for being there for me. Thank you for helping me shape the truth about myself.

You shouldn't have to travel far to find them. Behind the eyes that read this book, behind the breaths you hear as you peruse these pages, behind the rhythmic heartbeat that forms the soundtrack of this story, lies the one who has and will shape the love that that you possess for yourself and others.

That special someone who is in your corner to push you from better to best. That someone who can love you better than any other human being. That person is **Her**. She sets the standard for any other to present themselves to you. **Her**. Her tone tells people how to treat you and dismisses those who will not comply. She is you and these are the little lessons to live by while ***Becoming Her***.

"You yourself, as much as anybody in the entire universe, deserve your love and affection."
- Buddha

Chapter 1

We spend our whole lives looking for love. As little girls, we dream of partnership and marriage. I don't know about you, but when I was little and one of my favorite cousins came over, we played "husband and wife". I would cook the imaginary food, drive the imaginary kids in my imaginary van, and go to the imaginary grocery store. My perception of purpose was to have a husband and to be a wife.

When I grew older I was met with the reality that life would not happen as sweetly. Men wouldn't agree to be a husband as easily as one of my cousins did. Relationships would be laced with the desire and the competition to be accepted. There would be an exchange of words that could send you on a flight to cloud nine or on a train to the darkest corner of hell. Conveniently I would always remember the train ride, but never the flight when a person decided to exit my life.

My love was good. It was golden. I'd practiced for this part many times, many years ago. I couldn't understand how someone else could not appreciate it. It became my obligation to convince people why I should be loved. I poured out my love and acts of kindness for everyone. People took it because it was free. Still, that didn't mean that it was valued by anyone.

Later in life I discovered that the real secret to loving someone else without depleting myself was learning to love myself first. People often mention it, but how to do it is not always understood. If you have not taken the time to speak into yourself, to develop your thinking, and to surround yourself with people who help you grow, you should start right there.

Becoming Her 101: Lesson #1

Love yourself as hard as you have been trying to love others. It's your problem and your solution. You're looking for love and when people see how you love yourself, they will know how to love you in return

"Self-trust is the first secret of success."

-Ralph Waldo Emerson

Chapter 2

When I was little, I wanted to be a ballerina just like those of Alvin Ailey. I'd prance all over the living room until I was tired of jumping. I practiced weekend after weekend perfecting my little dream.

Needless to say, I'm not a ballerina today. As a matter of fact, I don't even like to dance because I'm so bad at it. When in the world did I discover that I'd never measure up to my Alvin Ailey dreams? It was probably the minute someone laughed at me for doing a routine wrong. Or maybe when I didn't get picked for Varsity cheerleading because dance was involved.

Either way, what I believed was possible changed the more my actions didn't measure up. Often this is what we do to ourselves. We aspire, and if we don't get good results, the aspiration diminishes.

Here's the thing. Some things come natural to us and others we'll have to practice to master. There may be moments of repeated failure even after we've been practicing. The saying, "behind every successful person are many failures", is a very real statement.

Failure can be so painful. It causes us embarrassment when we were hoping to deliver a stellar outcome but miss the mark.

The truth about failure, pain, and embarrassment is that it produces even greater results than what we planned when we were trying to succeed. It helps us grow. It teaches us how resilient we can be and how there really are more opportunities to start again. It offers a residual lesson of much-needed humility once it runs its course.

I'm not sure who invented the idea to run away from failure, but I say do the opposite. Be aware that you may fail, but fail with the expectancy of gaining something instead of losing. The only way to start being great is to start, no matter what.

Becoming Her 101: Lesson #2

Everything that you've ever done is the result of an attempt. Even when you are messing up, you are learning and becoming better. If you quit, the only thing you are becoming is a serial quitter. Always be able to count on yourself to give your best.

"The most important opinion you have of yourself, and the most significant things you say all day are those things you say to yourself."

—Unknown Author

Chapter 3

My sons used to make fun of me for talking to myself all the time. To this day, I have full-fledged conversations with myself. It's my way of rehearsing how I will verbally present to the world on a regular basis.

The large age gap between me and my siblings taught me how to imagine friends instead of actually having them. Even after my brothers and sister were born, the habit never left me.

Before coaching a client or speaking at an event, I get in the mirror or in my car and begin to have a conversation as if I am already in that moment. I anticipate how a person may respond and I reply accordingly. It sounds crazy I know.

When I do this, it allows me to be aware of my feelings, gain clarity in my thoughts and perceptions, and decrease the likelihood of being caught off guard with my emotions and words. But the best part about the conversations that I have with myself, is that before I pour into anyone else, I've spoken a good word over the most valuable person, me.

There is no point in dedicating my life to uplifting others if I haven't had a kind word with myself. You would be surprised at how much self-confidence you will have if you practice saying beautiful things to other people, but say them to yourself first.

When I speak to a woman to encourage her, I am absolutely convinced that my affirmations and advice are the law. I spoke it into myself first and it made me feel warm and excited. It made me even more excited to share the great news with someone else.

Sometimes, or all the time if you are like me, we must have the conversations with ourselves that someone else may not be able to have with us. '*Yes, I was created with a purpose. I am loved. I am strong. I've made mistakes, but I can see my progress. My best and brightest days are still ahead of me and because of that I will move forward and finish strong.*'

Go ahead, turn up the volume on what your soul needs to hear. After all, we become what we believe.

Becoming Her 101:

Lesson # 3

If hurt people, hurt people, then what do loved people do? Loving yourself first allows you to love others effectively. Tell yourself daily how much you love yourself and why. You were created from love and you were created to love. It is ok to tell yourself how much you love you.

"Someone else' s
opinion of you
does not have to
become your reality."
- Les Brown

Chapter 4

Before I met the love of my life, I dated a guy whose mom hated me. Like most mothers, she thought the world of her son. She also thought that I was not good enough for him. She'd mentioned that she envisioned her son with a lawyer or a doctor and I was neither.

During the period of being connected to that woman, her opinion of me always stuck in the back of my mind. I found myself miserable in my relationship and over-compensating by volunteering to help or engage in different functions to get her approval. Of course, I was never accepted.

The relationship ultimately failed. There were several factors that contributed to the decline (it just wasn't my destiny for one thing). Once again I'd managed to fail, but in this failure I granted myself a passport to live beyond the borders of someone else's opinion.

Moving forward, I took a valuable lesson with me. At no time in life did I have to own what another person chose to think of me. I also was not obligated to perform any differently than my authentic self. It was only my responsibility to conduct myself according to the standard of greatness that I know God placed inside of me.

This belief provided a huge acceleration in the direction of confidence, joy, and more meaningful relationships. The saying "be true to thine own self" now had clarity. Those who didn't like me were free to depart my life at the nearest exit. It didn't mean that I would be angry, but it didn't mean that I would rewrite the script for someone else either. What it did mean was that I was aware of my value and the price would not be altered just because someone's opinion differed.

We celebrate our freedom, yet we voluntarily make ourselves prisoner to the thoughts and feelings that others have towards us. We allow how the world sees us and what people say about us to determine our self-worth. Then we live our life according to that price tag while starving for attention, being depressed, harboring self-limiting beliefs, and having low self-esteem. We find ourselves totally dismissing how wonderful and capable we really are.

When was the last time you took inventory of all your divine greatness and worth? You were created wonderfully. You are one of one. There are no identical fingerprints, brain, or set of teeth.

Do great things in the world! Go back and remember who you are and whose you are.

Becoming Her 101: Lesson #4

Every day, make a deposit into your self-worth account. Speak over yourself. 'I am wonderful. I am beautiful. I am special. I am loved. I was created uniquely and specifically. I don't share every talent that others may have, but I am talented according to my own gifts.' Doing this reminds you of your value daily, just in case someone tries to persuade you otherwise.

"Don' t accept negative energy. Change it!"
-Tiffany Lewis

Chapter 5

My slight addiction to social media has afforded me the opportunity to hear the myriad of thoughts of other people. My friend list is mostly comprised of positive people or at least people who appear to be positive. There are a few questionable connections out of the bunch that I may have known from high school, with eccentric thoughts or behavior, but generally, they are mostly positive.

After scrolling daily past what seemed to be a million memes and another million thoughts, I came across a post that said: "Positive Vibes Only". The graphics were attractive and the quote made me totally agree with the post. There is enough struggle in the world like working jobs we hate, trying to watch our weight, or wanting to join the juicing diet, but we just finished eating a piece of fried chicken. I mean, who wants to be around a Negative Nancy all the time? A Positive Vibe movement was what my life needed.

On day one I looked for every social media friend that didn't have positive energy. I wanted them gone. As I scrolled through my page I saw a girl who I'd known for years. Her posts were mostly negative and downright annoying. I remember thinking, *why is your life so darn ugly*? I definitely wanted to delete her! Ironically, at the same time, she saw me online and sent me an instant message. The message read:

Her: *Hi Tiffany!*

Me: *Hi there!*

Her: *I just wanted to tell you that I just love reading your posts. You have really grown into a beautiful woman. You help keep me going. I'm going to get there one day!*

Me: *Awww. Thank you so much! I hope you continue to become inspired.*

Instantly my attitude changed and the "Positive Vibe Movement" was over. It was not because I didn't want to be surrounded by good people, but because I have the responsibility of delivering good into bad places. Just because people don't perform to the standard that we desire, does not mean that we stop performing good works.

How beneficial is what you have to offer to someone who already has it? Sure, positivity met with positivity breeds very favorable conditions, but negativity met with positivity can be life changing for you and someone else! There is a difference in looking good and being good. When being good is who you are and not just what you do or how you look, that is a power that you own. Negativity has the potential to change your mood, but it should not change your character.

Perception and positivity are ultimately controlled by you. Others may have negative words and actions, but how you respond to them is totally up to you. Don't allow people to pull you into their storm, simply pull them into your peace.

Becoming Her 101: Lesson #5

Light is the only way to eliminate darkness. The darkness is necessary for us to appreciate the light. Wherever you go, don't just look for the light, be the light in dark places. If things are not looking positive, use your power to change the view.

"From far away even giants look like ants."
-Tiffany Lewis

Chapter 6

Have you ever seen one of those movies where the girl's lover has gone away to war and it's uncertain if he'll ever return? What usually happens is one day she looks out into the distance and she sees something moving, but it's too small to make out who or what it could possibly be. Then after minutes of refocusing her lenses, the old lover is in plain sight, tired from running and panting for water. If that's too far-fetched, what about when you've watched a huge aircraft take off and after several minutes of upward travel it appears as if it's the size of a pea?

Either way, I find it amazing that time and distance can change the view of almost everything. This includes the direction of your life, your goals, and your dreams. We look around at others -a public figure or even our peers - and it makes us wonder how Jessica from way back is now on top. How in the world did she get there when you both started from the same place? She's doing big things and living large and in charge!

I've definitely made the critical mistake of comparing my timing of success to other people. And just as sure as the sky is blue, I was frustrated every time. It was self-defeat at its finest.

The truth is, you cannot measure your success by the success of others. In its perfect time, everything that is due to you will come. What you see others doing does not discredit what you are destined to do.

Just because someone is doing something on a larger scale at a different moment than you only means that right now is their appointed time. When the time is right, with faith and work, you will arrive at your destination.

When that pea-sized plane that we spoke of earlier finally lands, you no longer see what appeared to be tiny, but a massive aircraft. It's huge up close.

Just the same, you may be surrounded by people who are doing big things, but that doesn't mean you are not just as big. In due season, when the world can view you up close instead of watching you from afar, you will realize that all along you were a giant with enormous purpose. From a distance, even giants look like ants.

Becoming Her 101: Lesson #6

Patience is a virtue and you are purposed to do great things. Where you want to be is where you will be when you've put in the work. Everything has a process and a due date.
Until your due date, do great.
Your time is coming!

"Chase the purpose and the paper will chase you."

- Dean Lewis

Chapter 7

Through my years of being a coach, I've realized that people waste so much time on the unimportant. That which we call "reality TV" has helped to rearrange our values from self-love to selfie love. Ratchet behavior produces ratings and everything you've ever believed in has been compromised for notoriety and a check. Having your name recognized has become equivalent to success with no regard to whether the attention is negative or positive.

Now don't get me wrong, I love a nice bag, a clean ride, and even a cute selfie, but at the end of the day my actions and decisions need to line up with my destiny. Yes, it's my hope that people recognize my name and my work, but by that same desire, I share the responsibility of making sure that what people recognize me for will allow them to help themselves and others.

Success is a primary goal for us all, but what we choose to measure it with is the key. A cup will keep water contained. A sifter will not. Using the wrong tools will give us the wrong idea. There will be so many victories in our lives that we will miss if we are using the wrong standard to measure our success.

We are all given a talent that is not only useful to ourselves, but useful to others. Although there are some that may share our talents, we each have a specific gift that enhances our talents and allows it to be unique. There are hundreds of hairstylists, but your ability to adhere to time could be a discipline that allows you to set yourself apart from others. There are many vocalists, but your breathing technique may allow you to hold notes longer than another singer.

The desperate need for attention is not necessary for your success. Many share your talent, but your gift belongs to you. Pay more attention to how you impact others instead of how much money you can accumulate. What you will find is that you may be inspiring many before the masses even know your name.

Focus on what you are purposed to do. This will keep you in alignment with your morals. If “the love of money is the root of all evil”, chasing it is surely guaranteed to take you into places you never belonged.

Becoming Her 101:
Lesson #7

Your soul is housed within your body. Money can buy things for the body, but do what is good for the soul. How we develop on the inside helps what we display on the outside. What you are full of you can share with others. Find your purpose, share it with others and the money will come because your gift belongs to you.

"Life is measured in moments, make a lot of good ones."

-Tiffany Lewis

Chapter 8

One of the greatest things I believe my mother and grandmother gave me growing up were moments. We didn't always have much money but we sure shared lots of memorable time together.

From picnics and bike rides, to weekend vacations or just being able to lick the spoon after the cake batter was mixed, the memory of those moments has never left me.

As I got older I experienced many challenges in life. Teenage pregnancy, a struggle with alcohol use, and even homelessness. That period marked some of my darkest days. It was very difficult to comprehend how I would be able to get back on my feet again. I'd created a lifestyle for myself that was not conducive to success; not as a mother or as a woman.

There was one time when my children and I had to take residence at an extended stay hotel. It was drug infested in a side of town that was less than safe. Addicts would knock on my door and try to sell me miscellaneous things for money, like underwear, a fan, or whatever they could get their hands on in exchange for cash.

There would also be a peculiar group of men who were thought to be the security for the grounds. They would meet every night on the top floor of the two-story facility. Peering through the window, I would see different people getting shoved and punched into a unit. It was so sad, but I would go back to minding my business and tending to my children. I never understood what was going on there, but after while it began to seem normal to me.

If you become too comfortable with failure you will soon forget that you are failing. I was not failing because I had to live there. My failure was hidden behind the idea that I had to stay there when it was never my destiny. It began to seem as though the things occurring around me were not detrimental to the well-being of myself or my sons.

There were three people, one room, one bed, and one bath. Once I tried to date a guy who had no idea where I lived. I can recall him asking, "How come your children never go to their room?" It had never crossed my mind that my circumstances could seem so unusual to some until that point.

Although there were many other memories throughout my life that were more painful, I've learned to duplicate the moments that brought me joy and to continue to allow the painful moments to teach me to move in the opposite direction of the decisions that helped me to get there. I've learned that in the midst of my pain, I did not die. Pain can't kill you, but choosing not to deal with it could lead to death – the death of your dreams, the death of your hope, and the death of your destiny because you confused the situation and refused to act.

Now my days are filled with creating the same happy moments for my children. The world will issue them their own struggles based on their decisions which they must deal with. As much as I would like to save them from them all, I know it will not make them resilient and confident in their own abilities.

Even in their darkest days, they will have the light of the moments I worked to create for them to help guide the way. Life is measured in moments. Make a lot of good ones to help light the way during dark times.

Becoming Her 101: Lesson #8

Decisions will ultimately dictate the direction of your destiny. Decide to be aware that everything you do will either help you or hinder you. Live every moment deeply, full of gratitude and in the awareness that you are sprinkling light. When you look back on your little sprinkle of lights, you will realize you have created enough lights to see your way through the rest of the journey.

"Loving yourself is a journey with no deadline."

- Vision (Poet)

Chapter 9

Self-esteem or the lack thereof was the reason I started my company Becoming Her. One of the key factors behind why lots of women were not reaching their full potential was because they struggled with how they viewed themselves and their abilities. Since I'd shared the same struggles before, I felt it was my duty to help other women come out of this.

Even when you dress in the nicest clothes and drive the finest cars, if you are unable to see and appreciate all the qualities that make you amazing, it is more difficult to function in the absence of material things.

We all come so full of dreams and ideas about how life is supposed to be. The media, our friends, family, and just people in general, help shape our self-perception. For the longest time when I was a teenager, I had this idea that things were good but that I needed to be a little prettier, maybe lighter-skinned, my hair a little longer. I needed to be on the drill team instead of a cheerleader, and our house needed to be a little bigger than the small space that my mom had. I struggled with interacting with my peers because of these ideas. I found myself falsifying information (basically LYING) about what I had, what I knew, and what I had done in life.

The beginning of my lying was also the beginning of my never-ending chase after a fictitious person instead of understanding all the elements that made me unique. I easily became dissatisfied with everything about my life. I was young and depressed with a bad attitude! The negative opinions of others did further damage to my self-esteem and before long I'd officially self-taught unloving myself.

We are naturally born to love. Self-hate is a learned behavior. From pictures in magazines and our favorite reality-tv star, it is easy to mimic poor, but popular habits and superficial standards. We magnify what we are missing and minimize who we really are.

Love is what we were created from and is also what we are created for. When age allows, we begin pursuing relationships to fulfill this desire to love and to be loved, but some of us skip the step of loving ourselves first.

It seems easier to pour our idea of love into others hoping that it will inspire them to do the same. When that person fails us in love, it leaves broken pieces that are carried into the next relationship with the desire for that new person to be successful in repairing them.

The truth about love is that while we all need it; we all don't express it the same way. Some of the people in the most need of love have a tendency to do some of the most unloving things.

Spending time with yourself is imperative. It helps you to discover what you like, what you don't like, what hurts you, and what makes you feel good. It gives you the chance to evaluate you. It provides the opportunity to find out what you think of yourself without the clothes, makeup, and compliments of others. It gives you moments to celebrate all that you are in private and makes aware of all the things about you that still need to be perfected.

It is so much easier for someone to love you correctly when you are familiar with how to love yourself. Even when you find someone to love you in the way that you should be loved, you owe it to yourself to honor you, nurture you, and love you. As long as you live, you are responsible for loving you no matter what.

Becoming Her 101: Lesson #9

Say affirmations to yourself. Reward yourself. Take care of yourself. Forgive yourself. Push yourself. Be yourself. Most of all, never stop loving yourself. You were made from love and you were created to love.

"Everything does not require your energy."

-Tiffany Lewis

Chapter 10

Your personal energy consists of your thoughts, emotions, comments, and actions. I believe that if I had known how valuable my energy was long ago, I never would have wasted it on so many different people and situations.

Now that I'm older I realize that misjudging the value of my own energy caused me to inflate the value of others. Almost anyone needed to get a piece of my mind if they'd wronged me. Heck, if they'd done something wrong to someone I knew, they needed a piece of my mind! When someone was upset with me I felt that I must respond.

If I couldn't respond I would spend countless hours worrying about what went wrong and how I could fix it, no matter who was at fault. Those periods would usually end with me being exhausted and stressed out. Many times, my worrying produced no reconciliation. The process of overexerting my energy and ending up stressed about a situation became cyclic. I remember my aunt saying to me one day, "If you keep giving everyone a piece of your mind, you're not going to have any left." That was a little nugget she'd been learning herself. She was so right.

Today all I can say is experience is a very rigorous, but effective teacher. Stress is not just an overflow of emotion; it is an overflow of emotion which begins to manifest physically. It's a direct effect of how you choose to perceive and respond to situations. It is a process overloaded with side effects and it is not your friend. From my current perspective, it is a misuse of your energy.

If Popeye's sold a 2-piece snack for $25 would you buy it? I certainly would not. It is not reasonable. For that cost, I could use my money for so much more, and I love Popeye's! (I am trying to quit this habit, I promise.) Two pieces of chicken shoved in a box with a biscuit wrapped in paper does not hold a $25 value. At least put it on a plate with a real fork and some sides before you try to convince me that your product is valued at $25.

Do you understand where I am going with this? Your energy, the way you feel, your well thought out response, and your decision to act have high value! What you do or say can impact someone's life. What you do or say will also impact your own life. Great decisions can allow you to run your day with confidence or poor decisions can cause the day to run you and eventually they will determine the direction of your life.

Everyone is not prepared to receive your energy. Sometimes your silence will say enough. Sometimes your absence will do the same. It does not mean we withhold our great power from everyone. It means that we become intentional with sharing it. It makes us question our motives.

Do I speak up because this cause affects me and/or others or do I just want people to hear my point of view? Do I debate with my husband about this topic because it affects our well-being or because I want to be right?

When I began to question my motives and check myself, it became progressively easy to understand that not everything required my energy. I do not have to infuse myself into every situation. Many things will eventually work themselves out and those things that can't may just have to be worked out by a power greater than my own.

Becoming Her 101: Lesson #10

Choose whom you share your valuable energy with. Daily, practice patience, kindness, and goodness. Always be willing to pour into others, but never allow people and situations to deplete you. You have nothing to pour into others if you are empty.

"You can look at what you lost or look at what you have left."

-Tiffany Lewis

Chapter 11

Loss. Years ago I would have sworn that word meant Tiffany. Losing was the trend for my life during a certain period of time and I absolutely began to feel like a loser.

In one year alone I lost my apartment, my boyfriend, my truck, I was robbed, and I lost my peace of mind to my first experience with domestic violence.

It so easy to begin to believe that you've been set up to fail when the odds are consistently stacked against you. No matter how hard I tried to take two steps forward I'd always end up taking three steps backward. Before long, I'd pretty much given up on trying to do the right thing because the wrong things just seemed to come to me much easier.

The company I kept was full of the perfect ingredients to have me tangled up in a life run by money, sex, and alcohol. Street drugs were never my thing, but I did become addicted to having fun and fast money, since losing had taken me into the pits of depression.

My new job waitressing at the strip club afforded me all the material stuff I wanted. I slept all day and the work that felt more like play, I did by night.

Meeting new people became my new hobby and a man with plenty of money was my new friend. Dinner dates, vacations, and marriage proposals became my norm.
At twenty something what more did a girl need? All that losing had come to an end, or so I thought.

My time with my children was almost non-existent. I stayed up long enough in the mornings from work to get them off to school, but I was usually tired when they got home. I needed a nap during the day to work a 9 to 5; P.M. to A.M., that is. After months of being on "top of the world," my body was wearing down. Even on days off I could not function to do typical things like go to church because my sleeping schedule was so off track.

After a while, the loud music became annoying, the attention was overwhelming, and everything I'd signed up for I no longer wanted.

Still, being addicted to material things and going from nothing to something made it very difficult to make a change. I stuck with the routine, but internally I was struggling. I wanted a normal life, but I didn't want to give up how I was doing things. I plastered on makeup and a smile night after night while the rest of the world passed me by during the day. I was still losing.

One night, I was raped while on a date. I never told a soul until I married my husband. I felt it came with the lifestyle I had chosen. I was so broken on the inside because I knew that this life had nothing more to offer me, but my fear of losing the material made me stick to what I knew did not serve me.

I never returned to the club after that. For some time, there was no money in my pockets or nice new shoes and clothes. With the help of others however, there was a roof over my head where I could sit at a table and help my children with homework. Fast forward more than 10 years and my teenage boys always tell me how they didn't know we were without so many things. They were just glad to be with me.

Just when I thought I had lost everything all over again, I could finally see that what I'd lost was never a big deal, but what was left was so much more important.

Becoming Her 101: Lesson #11

There are some things that can only be lost if you choose to shut your soul off from its gift, like love, joy, peace and hope. Focus on these things. Even in the absence of material things, you will always have the opportunity to experience an abundance of the things that matter most.

"You are only going to go as far as your discipline will take you."

-Heavy D

Chapter 12

My husband is an entrepreneur. While I was dating him we often talked business. He is always on time, if not early. He keeps a briefcase of his barbering tools in his trunk and mine! If he's ever called at the last minute to work, he's always prepared. He once told me his favorite quote is "proper preparation prevents poor performance". He absolutely lives by that.

Well honey, let me be the first to tell you that his wife is the exact opposite. I'm always rushing. I stress myself out by never being fully prepared and doing several things off the cuff. Although it creates more stress than I can handle sometimes, I'd managed to become successful in the corporate world. Winging it worked for me until I got married. The joy and contentment that was reflected in my husband's life made me a little angry. He was always happy and ready to defeat the day while I was always grumpy and annoyed and the day would mostly defeat me.

I'd watch him in disappointment and try to figure out why in the world I could not be like him. One day I finally figured it out. The difference between the two of us is discipline. He despises the effect that poor performance will have on his day so he does whatever it takes to be prepared.

Procrastination is not a belief of his. He lives by "why not now?".

Procrastination is a dirty little thief if you didn't know. It will always convince you that there is more time. It will reason with you if you think you're too tired, too afraid, or not good enough. It will empty you of every reason why you should, until you haven't. For just as much as you have to do, procrastination will have just as many excuses.

Before long it will latch on and be an extension of you. When you look around you, notice that there was plenty of opportunity, but procrastination lied its way into your space.

This is exactly why I could not mirror the traits of my husband when it came to business. You must have a full understanding that procrastination is your enemy. Think about an enemy you may have had when you were in high school. When you knew they would be at the party or the football game, you came prepared! Come on now, you know! Your hair was laid and you had on the cutest clothes and shoes.

Let's not forget your crew. If your enemy was going to be there you had to have at least one best friend around in case she tried some funny business.

You must treat procrastination the same way. The best way to beat it is to be prepared. Being prepared takes discipline. I had to learn (and I'm still learning truthfully) that if I wanted to go far I had to beat my enemy. That means getting clothes out the night before. It means waking up one to two hours early. It means writing a plan and sticking to it. It also means understanding that there may be more time, but right now is my time.

Eventually the steps you take to discipline yourself will no longer be what you do, but who you are. Your new habit will become so life changing for you. Discipline and success are best friends. I tell myself this every time I feel myself about to procrastinate. I want the best for myself and I know that you do too.

Push through! Go the extra mile and take the extra steps. Your successful self will thank you later.

Becoming Her 101: Lesson #12

Discipline and success are best friends. Say this to yourself. When you put in the work the universe will meet you the rest of the way.

"Little white lies will become big black pits that you will eventually fall into."
-Tiffany Lewis

Chapter 13

High school was a very challenging time for me. More specifically, freshman and sophomore year. I entered ninth grade at a new school because we'd recently moved away from the neighborhood that I'd grown up in. I didn't know anybody but making friends was not so difficult for me as I was pretty outgoing. I did have somewhat of a smart mouth so I would consider myself a love me or hate me kind of girl, depending on your personality. If you were sensitive or very literal, my sarcasm would most likely not amuse you. I was slender with a baby face unlike other girls my age who were fully developed.

I was also very juvenile for 15. I was the only child for ten years and I still owned a Barbie playhouse and played with it from time to time. To my surprise, high school was nothing like I expected. No one was talking about the newest Barbie and training bras were out of the question.

I'd been a cheerleader at the park for years so joining the cheerleading squad helped me make friends. All the boys began to notice me so I made friends with the girls on my squad at least. I quickly came up to speed with high school life. There was just one thing I had not quite graduated to however...sex. I mean for crying out loud I'd only kissed a boy 3 times by ninth grade!

With my new found high school personality came my real interest in boys. On my school bus route was one of the cutest football players I'd ever seen. We'll call him Ron. On that same bus was one of the most promiscuous, most overly developed girls I'd ever met. She had boobs the size of my mother's and she knew how to use them! We'll call her Jenny. Jenny was on my cheerleading squad. There was no child in the whole school built like her. She wasn't very pretty in the face in my opinion, but the boys didn't seem to care. She was definitely having sex. Most of our conversations were about clothes, cheerleading, and sex.

I learned that if I wanted to keep up with high school conversation I'd better start talking like I knew about sex and having one thing I had not quite graduated to however...sex. I mean for crying out loud I'd only kissed a boy 3 times by ninth grade!

With my new found high school personality came my real interest in boys. On my school bus route was one of the cutest football players I'd ever seen. We'll call him Ron. On that same bus was one of the most promiscuous, most overly developed girls I'd ever met. She had boobs the size of my mother's and she knew how to use them! We'll call her Jenny. Jenny was on my cheerleading squad. There was no child in the whole school built like her. She wasn't very pretty in the face in my opinion, but the boys didn't seem to care. She was definitely having sex. Most of our conversations were about clothes, cheerleading, and sex.

I learned that if I wanted to keep up with high school conversation I'd better start talking like I knew about sex and having pretty outgoing. I did have somewhat of a smart mouth so I would consider myself a love me or hate me kind of girl, depending on your personality. If you were sensitive or very literal, my sarcasm would most likely not amuse you. I was slender with a baby face unlike other girls my age who were fully developed.

I was also very juvenile for 15. I was the only child for ten years and I still owned a Barbie playhouse and played with it from time to time. To my surprise, high school was nothing like I expected. No one was talking about the newest Barbie and training bras were out of the question.

I'd been a cheerleader at the park for years so joining the cheerleading squad helped me make friends. All the boys began to notice me so I made friends with the girls on my squad at least. I quickly came up to speed with high school life. There was just some. I managed to get through the entire first half of the year without losing my virginity, but it was becoming hard. Ron had a girlfriend and didn't pay me much attention as a love interest, but other football players were after me.

I lied so much during that year it was ridiculous. I'd say that I couldn't sleep with them because I was sleeping with my boyfriend who lived across town. In reality, I'd been molested for years and sexual stuff just made me nervous.

I eventually ended up with a boyfriend named Clinton. He was a senior and of course, a football player. He was very kind and patient with me. I'll never forget. I never felt pressured by him and he always treated me with respect. Still, I never lost my virginity to him although I know that he was patiently waiting for the prize.

When the second semester came, my lie became true. I'd lost my virginity to a childhood friend that lived across town and not to Clinton. I'd finally been swallowed up by all the sexual pressure. It made returning to school even more difficult. Now that I was experienced I had even more conversations with boys and Clint began to hate the rumors he was hearing. They were all lies but not very flattering to be attached to such a dignified young man. We broke up.

With Clint out of the way, I now aggressively pursued Ron. One day he got off at my stop and came to my house. We made out but I realized I was still very afraid of sex and Ron ended up leaving.

The next day when I saw Jenny, I told a lie that she was not to repeat. She'd said she wanted Ron, but I wanted him for myself. So I told her that I'd slept with him and it was horrible, hoping to deter her. When I arrived at school the next day everyone was staring at me. Jenny told Ron and he was pissed! He made a fool of me that day. He cursed me out in front of a group of friends and spread every evil rumor about me to be sure to ruin my life and in my book, it was truly ruined.

I struggled so much at home just being a teenager and keeping that huge secret from my mom about being molested. Now school was just as big a mess. I was so embarrassed by my reputation that I stopped all extracurricular activities.

My grades declined and I began entertaining any guy that was nice to me at school. I never lived up to all the rumors that were said about me, but I was no saint after that either. I made some pretty bad decisions. My name traveled through the county and people that didn't even know me talked about me.

Now that I'm an adult I realize that if I'd started with the truth, it would have taken me so much farther. I never had to live up to their standards. My standards were high so instead, I brought myself down. I hurt myself. I ruined my self-esteem and my pride. It took me forever to rebuild my confidence. My little white lies followed me a very long way.

Becoming Her 101: Lesson #13

Honesty is the best policy. If it seems difficult to tell the truth you should pay attention to your actions. What you do should always align with who you are. If they don't, you're not just telling a lie, you're living a lie.

"Always be prepared for your moment."- Mariah Huq

Chapter 14

When you think of your dreams for yourself what do you see? How do you see yourself? Be specific. Now based on that vision, if I met you tomorrow and presented you with the opportunity to live out your dreams would you be ready?

I've always wanted to be a writer and a life coach. The first time someone basically sat the opportunity to live out my dreams in front of me, I was not ready. Since high school I'd worked in the dental field. Eventually, I worked my way up to office manager. For fifteen years I worked in that field until one day a lady came to bring her husband to the dentist.

She was a published author with a publishing company. She accompanied her husband to his dental visit and while she waited for him to be seen, she approached me and asked if I knew anyone that had written a book or would like to write a book. It was right around the time that I was tired of my job and sat daydreaming about being a famous coach and writer. I'd begun creating a following on social media, but had not done much. I immediately told her yes, me, and invited her into my office to elaborate.

She told me about a writer's workshop that she was hosting. It would coach me through the writing process over a certain number of weeks and even publish my book at the end of the course. I was super excited, but afraid. I was certain that I would not be able to afford the cost of the class because I was a single mother. Sure enough, it was financially out of my league.

The lady and I talked during her husband's entire appointment. By the end of our conversation she told me that I was so inspiring that I needed to be a writer and she would pay my tuition! I was blown away! Money seemed to be the only thing ever holding me back.

A few weeks later I began the course. What I didn't know is that it took way more for me to be successful at this than just money. It required my focus, sacrifice, discipline, and determination.

I tried going through the course, but never disciplined myself enough to stay on time with it. After the allotted time, the course was over and with missed assignments and even missed classes, I had not finished the work. I'd missed my moment and taken for granted the gift that this woman extended to me. I was so unprepared.

Each day it ate away at me that I'd failed to complete the task. Although I missed the opportunity at that time I learned a very valuable lesson when it was all said and done. Being prepared for your moment does not mean getting ready when the conditions look like they will be favorable. It means living in your dream even before the tables turn for your benefit. You have to walk in what you believe you will become before you have the funds, the resources, or the chance. Write before you are a writer, speak before you are a speaker, study medicine before you are a doctor and teach before you are a teacher. In perfect timing, the right moment becomes your moment.

Becoming Her 101: Lesson #14

Take your dream and develop it. Study it. Surround yourself with people who have accomplished it. Discipline yourself for what it takes to do it. Practice it even before it happens. Believe in it and believe in yourself.

"Fear does not stop death, but it can stop your life."
—Tiffany Lewis

Chapter 15

At age 7 my mother entered me into a beauty pageant. She wanted me to walk out smiling and waving with one hand on my hip. I was so mad. My mother knew good and well I was afraid of the crowd and waving at them would only make it worse. I didn't win that competition, but the judges ended up liking my mother's instructions for me. If she had not made me do it, I certainly would not have.

When I sit with my mom some days we reflect on how scary I used to be. Watching the clouds move across the sky made me cry. It sounds silly, but it's true. Now that I have my own children, they are about as scary as I was. They are not afraid of the clouds, but if I asked them to walk out at an event smiling and waving they would melt right out of their skin. The effects of childhood fears can easily overflow into your adult life and even your children's lives. Our society is structured in a way that will have you second guessing yourself and fearful that you are inadequate and don't fit the mold of popular opinion.

Fear is another little thief that will breed inactivity and rob you. So many people die with their dreams because they were too afraid to live them out. I started a business three times before this one and they all failed. As an honorary student in the school of failure, I know exactly how hard it can be to believe in yourself beyond failure. It's even hard to believe in yourself before you fail.

Bring the last time you failed back to memory. Did it hurt? Probably. Having children hurt like hell, but I had three! I'm still puzzled about how I managed to do that when having the first one scared the poop out of me. Ask yourself these 3 things before you decide to let fear run your life:

1. Is what I'm afraid of a fact, or a feeling that I'm afraid of?
2. If it's a fact, will it kill me if I confront it?
3. If I never face this fear will I live the life that I want and can I live out my purpose with the way that I am living now?

I've answered these questions many times and more often than not, the fear has been a feeling and never a fact. Once I conquered what I was afraid of, it was not so bad at all. As a matter of fact, I'd try it all over again.

There are enough dead dreams in the cemetery. Let yours live through you.

Becoming Her 101: Lesson # 15

Surrendering to fear is always optional.

"If you don't have
access to the elevator,
take the stairs."
-Tiffany Lewis

Chapter 16

Have you ever looked around and glanced at what appeared to be everybody succeeding but you? My journal is full of prayers from years ago begging God to please let it be my turn. Please help keep me from getting jealous and envious.

I always give my clients the advice to surround yourself with people who have done what you want to do. Here's a little transparency: it's much easier said than done at first.

It's one thing to become connected with professionals in your field that are already successful. Your expectations are high because that's why you were interested in the connection in the first place. But what about that friend that started from the bottom with you, just like you?

Suddenly her business is picking up, her social media following is crazy, and she's in the spotlight while you are still diligently working. You are happy for her, but your happiness is housed right across from your anxiety that you will never get there.

I used to absolutely hate that! I had to become aware of my problem. I wanted to go faster than the process would allow and it was messing me up. Take baking a cake for instance. You collect the ingredients, you combine, you mix, and then you bake. Now I'm a great cook, but a horrible baker so I believe we will bake the cake for about 25 to 35 minutes. (If that is incorrect please excuse my poor baking skills, but stick with me.)

If I remove the cake from the oven and halt the process of baking before my time is up, I will not have an edible cake. I will have mush. What I set out to do will not be fulfilled because I wanted to rush the process. The process that leads you into your purpose takes time.

Another problem I was having was not just rushing the process, but understanding the process as a whole. Your purpose in life will unfold in stages. Never discredit the stage that you are in. If you are putting in the work, then you must trust the process. Let's use the cycle of the butterfly as our next example.

Before we get to this beautiful creature we start with a fat, hairy worm. He slowly wobbles about in low places always at risk of being trampled beneath someone's foot. During this season, the caterpillar roams about, focused on his purpose doing the things that a caterpillar should, but he understands that before long he will be taking the next steps into his destiny. After all that time as a caterpillar, he is then isolated and shut off from the world in a cocoon. Experiencing a season of loneliness looks difficult to some, but the caterpillar is still focused on his destiny. For if it had given up because he could only be seen as a fat, hairy worm by others, or if being alone and isolated in a dark cocoon became too much and he emerged from it too soon, he would never have become a butterfly.

Your purpose has stages. Your purpose is wrapped in a process. You cannot judge where you are going by trying to measure someone else's process and progress. Stay focused on your destiny.

Sow the seeds to make your dreams grow and trust that in due time, what seemed too slow, or too ugly, or too dark, or too lonely, is directly tied to your destiny. If you stop too early you will miss where you are trying to go.

Becoming Her 101: Lesson #16

Celebrate the other butterflies in your life and stay focused with the faith that your time is coming.

"Be who you
once needed."
-Unknown

Chapter 17

In a radio interview I was once asked what advice I would give to my younger self. I don't remember what my response was exactly, but what I do know is that every year that I am alive the answer to that question changes.

Today I would answer that question by saying read this book, but to take make it more specific I would say a few things like this:

1. Growth can be hard. It requires commitment and the understanding that you may fail. Failure, however, fuels your growth. You can get it wrong many times, but one right is all you need.
2. Let the content of your character define your success. Personality is who we are around people, but character is who we are when no one is around. When your character directs you, your reward will not be solely based on how you perform, but you will be recognized by who you are.
3. You cannot change your destination overnight, but you can change your

direction overnight. Let go of the things that keep you from your full potential.

4. Feed your focus. The best way to eat an elephant is one piece at a time. Set goals, prioritize, and then crush them. Master focus instead of mastering multitasking. Multitasking may take you somewhere fast, but focus will take you far.
5. Your world is shaped by your choices, so make good ones. When you give your best you will receive the best, but just know that your best will be different each day.

Becoming Her 101: Lesson #17

*Read this section daily.
Rehearse it in real life
and repeat.*

"It' s never too late to
be what you might
have been."
-Tiffany Lewis

Chapter 18

When I was 25 I swore that at 40 I would retire from my job and open a small restaurant. I've always loved to eat, but didn't quite know how to cook. My siblings always tell me they remember how bad my cooking was when they were little. My mom worked late sometimes and cooking was up to me.

After a few years and lots of lessons from my grandmother and roommate, I really learned to cook.

Now I try to apologize to my brother and sister with succulent meals whenever they come to visit. With my little brother away at college, he is always ringing my phone asking me how to prepare something. Oh, how the tables have turned.

Even though I still love to cook and the idea of owning a restaurant sounds exciting to me, somehow I gave up on that dream. Being only five years short of 40, my dreams of becoming a life coach and author are just beginning to take off.

There is no way I will be able to own a restaurant, be a life coach and a chef too. I easily tucked away my ambitions since cooking for my family seemed sufficient.

One day, while speaking to a client who complained about her need for a life coach to help her with confidence in her mid-forties, I realized that her need resonated with me. My husband would often tell me, "you are a life coach, now coach yourself" and in the middle of this session, I had a self-coaching moment.

There are no rules to how many dreams a person can have. The only limitation is how many you decide to execute. So for my client, her need to work on confidence at this age was the maturation of her mindset. She understood that to get to the next level she would have to have more confidence.

For myself, did cooking or having a restaurant have to happen at 40? I can cook when I am 60 if I choose or 70 for that matter. I may find joy in teaching my children to cook well and allowing them to open the restaurant. There is no reason why a dream has to die with age. Even then, teaching your gifts to someone else and being a mentor is a sure way to see your dreams come to pass. You may not experience everything you would like to physically, but there are so many ways to make a dream come true. Just open your mind to the possibilities.

Becoming Her 101: Lesson #18

You always have a gift to offer the world. Don't limit your dreams by believing that you are the only one that can execute them. Share your gift with others. Being a mentor to someone else is like planting a seed. It will continue to grow even after the person that planted it is gone.

"Sometimes you just have to leap and build your wings on the way down."

-Kobi Yamada

Chapter 19

When I started Becoming Her all I had was an idea. When I started Becoming Her Jr. all I had was an idea. I knew that I wanted to help women and girls. I also knew that I wanted to offer them books, tools, and resources to feel empowered to live the best life possible. I knew nothing about the logistics.

All my days were spent on Google and social media. I followed anyone that did anything that looked remotely close to what I wanted to accomplish. After much research, I launched a website and 2 social media pages. I had not even created the products or content for my business. I just wanted a following. I advertised my life coaching packages by video and by offering a free consultation.

People were watching me, but I was not getting the traction that I needed to make my business go where I wanted to go. Since I was not getting the clientele or exposure that I needed to support my business, my website shut down twice. I couldn't afford it.

I went to networking events and didn't hand out business cards when I met people because I didn't want them to go to my defunct website. Man, I was really just faking it trying to make it.

While faking it until you make it can lead you to some great opportunities and people that will be able to help you accomplish your goals, you have to know what to do to make it and actually do it. Otherwise, you'll only end up faking it.

I had to learn that if I didn't have the tangible products to connect me with my target audience my business would be short lived. How will you establish credibility for yourself? People will listen to talk for a while, but in order to sustain you must produce. It is ok to be a dreamer, but execution is key. It was the very thing my business was missing. I was coming up with great ideas, but never seeing them to their completion. Faking will eventually become exhausting and you'll notice others around you will begin to take your ideas and make a fortune off them.

My notebooks, well my 5 notebooks, are flooded with ideas, but my portfolio of completed works was empty. Talk is cheap if you don't have a product to support it. Have a plan to make it before you begin faking it. You don't have to wait until all the pieces of the puzzle are there to begin. Just make sure that once you take the leap that you are prepared to build the wings on the way down.

Becoming Her 101: Lesson #19

Falling and flying are not the same thing. Position yourself to fly.

"You can't have a better tomorrow if you are still thinking about yesterday."

-Tiffany Lewis

Chapter 20

I wrote this book in hopes that it would bless somebody and change their life. In the process, it blessed me. While I think highly of myself, I am sometimes reminded of what I've been through and even my shortcomings.

This book required me to visit parts of my past to deliver my message in the most transparent way. While it hurt to be reminded of some of the choices I made, it felt good to be healed enough to share them with others in hope that they would find the lesson in it.

For many years, I was crippled by the many mistakes that I'd made throughout my life. I thought that no one other than God would see me fit enough to be anything more than a failure. Because of that fear, I held back my dreams for what seemed way too long. I stayed in relationships with some of the wrong people far beyond their expiration date. I'd totally decreased the value of who I was. Since I could not hide under a rock, I still had to push forward with my life and try to learn to live beyond my mistakes. That by far is the best thing that could have ever happened to me.

I learned that all my past errors looked as if they never belonged there, but I would never be able to reach my full potential without them. My mistakes were not just for me. They were to be compiled and saved in my memory bank to later be displayed to the many girls and women who have traveled down the same road. It is to remind them that they are not alone. It is to encourage them that failure is not final. It is to empower them to dust themselves off and to keep going.

No matter what has happened to you, I am a living witness that while your past may look like a setback, it is really a setup for your comeback. Your best and brightest days are still in front of you. If you haven't remembered anything from this book I would like for you to remember this:

You are special. You were uniquely designed to do a thing that only you can do in the way that you can do it. If you hoard your gift and never share it with the world, it is impossible for you to fulfill your purpose. Your past does not define you, it will help design you. There would be no way to appreciate the light if there were never dark days. You will become what you believe. If you have a hard time believing, say it until you see it. There is someone in the world counting on you to be the very light that they are in need of. The world is waiting on you and I am rooting for you. You have what it takes to be the best you because no one else has been created to be you other than you.

Love,

Tiffany

Becoming Her 101: Lesson # 20

Think of someone that you know and get them this book!

www.ingramcontent.com/pod-product-compliance
Lightning Source LLC
Chambersburg PA
CBHW051426090426
42737CB00014B/2850

9780692805442